Ecosystems of North America

The Pacific Coast

Maria Mudd Ruth

BENCHMARK BOOKS

MARSHALL CAVENDISH
NEW YORK

With thanks to Dr. Dan Wharton, Central Park Wildlife Center, for his careful reading of the manuscript.

Benchmark Books
Marshall Cavendish Corporation
99 White Plains Road
Tarrytown, New York 10591-9001

Library of Congress Cataloging-in-Publication Data
Ruth, Maria Mudd.
      The Pacific Coast / Maria Mudd Ruth
          p. cm. — (Ecosystems of North America)
      Included bibliographical references.
      Summary: Examines the tides, plants, animals, and ecosystems found along the Pacific coast from the icy waters of Alaska to the tropical waters of Mexico.
      ISBN 0-7614-0935-1
      1. Coastal ecology—Pacific Coast (North America)—Juvenile literature. [1. Coastal ecology—Pacific Coast (North America). 2. Ecology] I. Title. II. Series.
      QH104.5.P32 M84   2001   577.5'1'0979—dc21   00-020008

Photo Credits

Photo research by Candlepants, Inc.
Cover photo: Corbis © Ralph A. Clevenger
The photographs in this book are used by permission and through the courtesy of: Corbis: © Darell Gulin, 4–5, 43, 44; © Raymond Gehman, 9, 22–23; © Douglas P. Wilson/Frank Lane Picture Agency, 10; © Bob Rowan/Progressive Images, 13; © Gary Braasch, 14–15; © Kennan Ward, 16, 33; © W. Wayne Lockwood, M.D., 19, 30–31; © Wolfgang Kaehler, 21; © Kevin Fleming, 24; W. Perry Conway, 26; © Natalie Fobes, 29, 50, 52; © Jeffrey L. Rotman, 32; © Brandon D. Cole, 35; © Joel W. Rogers, 38–39; © George Lepp, 46–47, 49; © Craig Aurness, 54–55; © Jim Zuckerman, 56; © Staffan Widstrand, 58; © Jim Sugar Photography, 59; © Ric Ergenbright, back cover. Thomas Hamer: 41.

Printed in Hong Kong
6   5   4   3   2   1

Contents

The Edge of the Continent

North America's Pacific coast stretches from the icy arctic waters of Alaska to the warm, tropical lagoons of Mexico. It is where the Pacific Ocean meets the western edge of the North American continent. If you followed the coast in an airplane (or on the back of a seagull), you would travel about 4,000 miles (6,400 km). But the coast is not a straight line. It is so jagged that if you could straighten it out, it would measure more than 56,000 miles (94,640 km)—more than twice the distance around the world. Either way, your flight over the coast would reveal an endless series of wonders— glaciers, headlands, sand dunes, wide beaches, rocky coves, huge sea stacks, river mouths, protected bays, towering cliffs, and forested mountains growing right to the edge of the sea.

As you stand on a small sandy beach you might wonder where the coast exactly is. Is it where the water and the land come in contact? Does it extend out into the ocean or stretch inland past the beach or cliff? If so, how far? Because the coast is a transitional zone between the land and the ocean, it includes parts of the ocean, parts of the land, and a unique area that falls in between. The Pacific coast extends from the high-tide

Crashing waves and rugged, rocky headlands create a challenging environment along the Pacific coast. Yet the organisms here are bountiful, and the communities they form are of unparalleled diversity and beauty.

mark on the shoreline out to the water that lies above the continental shelf, the submerged land that borders the continent. The shelf varies in width, but averages about 40 miles (65 km) wide while the water that covers it averages about 200 feet (60 m) deep. This area is often referred to as the nearshore waters. Plants and animals living here are considered part of the marine world.

The coast also includes the inland area that is characterized by a mild, moist climate and ocean breezes, salt-laden air, often strong winds, and, in some areas, fog that forms over the ocean and moves inland. Plants and animals living on this portion of the coast are considered part of the terrestrial world. The coast also includes another area that falls between the marine and terrestrial worlds. It is the area along the coast that is alternately covered and uncovered by high and low tides. This area is called the **intertidal zone**. Plants and animals living here are exposed to air when the tide is low and submerged or splashed with water when the tide is high.

The Pacific coast is long and wide, but it is not a fixed boundary marking the land's end. It is constantly changing in an endless battle with the ocean. As the waves beat against the shore, the land changes, the sand shifts, and the cliffs crumble. This makes the Pacific coast a dynamic and exciting place to visit, but not an easy place for plants and animals to make their homes. They must meet the challenges of strong waves, fluctuating tides, changes in water temperature and salinity (saltiness), and often rough winter storms. In different ways, these plants and animals meet these challenges and make the Pacific coast a fascinating place to explore.

Coastal Communities

The vast Pacific coast offers plenty of space for a variety of **organisms**, or living things. But these organisms don't live just anywhere. They settle in particular **habitats**, or places that provide all the living and nonliving things an organism needs to survive. Organisms live where the food, climate, soil, water temperature, and other factors suit them

> In 1957, scientists discovered that marine birds that drink salt water have a gland above each eye that removes salt from the bird's bloodstream. The excess salt water is discharged from the gland through the nostril or mouth in head-shaking movements.

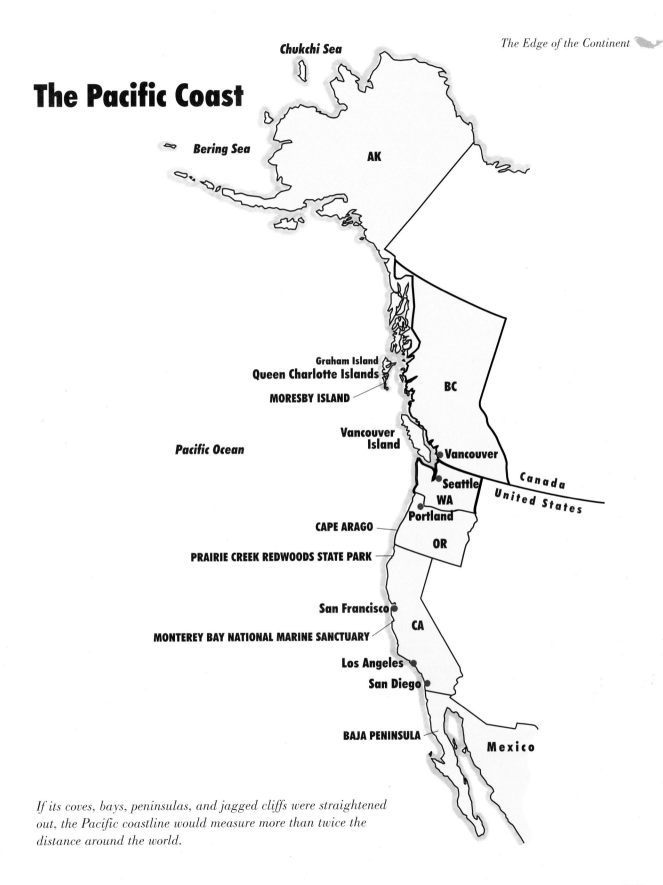

The Pacific Coast

Chukchi Sea

Bering Sea

AK

Graham Island
Queen Charlotte Islands

MORESBY ISLAND

BC

Vancouver Island

Pacific Ocean

● **Vancouver**

Canada

● **Seattle**
WA

United States

● **Portland**

CAPE ARAGO

OR

PRAIRIE CREEK REDWOODS STATE PARK

San Francisco ●

CA

MONTEREY BAY NATIONAL MARINE SANCTUARY

Los Angeles ●

San Diego ●

BAJA PENINSULA

Mexico

If its coves, bays, peninsulas, and jagged cliffs were straightened out, the Pacific coastline would measure more than twice the distance around the world.

best. A sea otter, for instance, needs to live in cold waters off the rocky coast near undersea forests of giant kelp, an algae we usually refer to as a seaweed. It also requires an abundant supply of food including urchins and abalone. So the sea otter makes its home wherever these foods thrive. Other animals move to new habitats to meet their needs during different stages of their lives. The habitats of the gray whale, for instance, include the cold nearshore waters off the coast of Alaska as well as the warm lagoons in Mexico. Salmon swim in the nearshore waters as adults and move into freshwater streams along the coast to lay their eggs. One species of seabird, the marbled murrelet, dives for fish in the ocean but nests in the treetops of coastal forests.

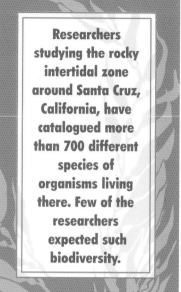

Researchers studying the rocky intertidal zone around Santa Cruz, California, have catalogued more than 700 different species of organisms living there. Few of the researchers expected such biodiversity.

Why does a whale need cold and warm water? Why can't the salmon lay its eggs in the ocean? How does the kelp aid the sea otter? How can all of these organisms share the same water? Many of these questions can be answered by a kind of scientist called an ecologist. **Ecology** is the study of the relationships among different species of plants and animals and their surroundings, or environment. The environment includes all the living and nonliving things around an organism. The environment of the kelp, for instance, includes the water it grows in, the rocks it anchors itself on, the temperature of the water, the amount of sunlight it receives, the nutrients in the water, and the hundreds of animals that live on it, hide in it, and eat it. To make survival in a particular habitat easier, different species of animals and plants interact with each other, forming **biological communities**. People live in communities of families, neighborhoods, towns, and cities for much the same reason. The Pacific coast holds many communities—some made up of many different species, other of just a few. Collectively, these various biological communities and their environments form the Pacific coast **ecosystem**.

Going with the Flow of Energy

Energy is the fuel that drives an ecosystem. In the Pacific coast ecosystem, as in all others, the ultimate source of energy is the sun.

Along the rocky coast of British Columbia, low tide exposes a constellation of sea stars—slow-moving but aggressive animals that play a dynamic role in the intertidal community.

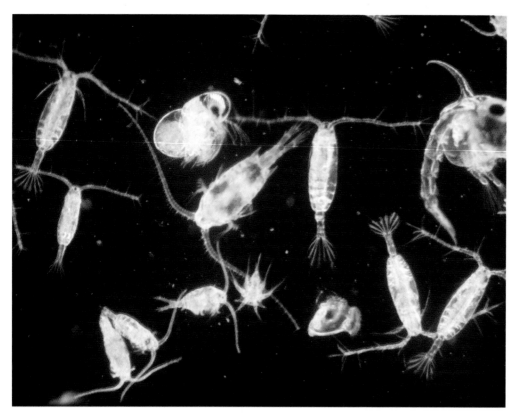

Microscopic animals and plants called plankton float and swim near the surface of the ocean water. Directly or indirectly, nearly all other marine creatures depend on these tiny life-forms as their food source.

But how does the sun's energy find its way into each and every living thing? It flows through a food chain. A **food chain** is a pathway that describes feeding relationships in which one organism is eaten by another, that is, in turn, eaten by another. Many food chains begin in the photic zone, the upper region of the ocean where the sunlight reaches. Here, microscopic single-celled algae called **phytoplankton** convert the sun's energy and the nutrients in the water into their own food through a process called **photosynthesis**. Some phytoplankton are consumed by tiny animals called zooplankton, which are not capable of photosynthesis. Zooplankton include the larvae, or immature forms, of many marine animals such as jellyfish, mollusks, and fish. The zooplankton are eaten by fish. When a bird swoops down to catch the fish, it is getting a share of the sun's energy that has

Sunlight Under Water

Through the process of photosynthesis, phytoplankton, kelp, and many other kinds of algae convert sunlight into energy. They live in the upper layer of the water as far down as the sunlight penetrates. How far the sunlight penetrates depends on how deep and clear the water is. This project will help you find out how far light can penetrate a body of water by making a simple version of a device used by ocean scientists. It is called a Secchi disc. NOTE: This project requires some simple hardware and the supervision of an adult. It is a project to do at the waterside. If you don't live near the ocean, you can make this Secchi disc and pack it with you when you go to the beach. You can also do the experiment at a lake or pond.

You will need:

- one end of a metal can measuring about 3 ½ inches (9.5 cm) across. (A coffee can or large tuna fish can are just about right)
- duct tape or masking tape
- an eye bolt
- two nuts and two washers to fit the eyebolt
- a hammer
- a large nail
- small amounts of black and white enamel paint
- a ruler or tape measure
- a strong cord 50 feet (15 m) long

1. Use the tape to cover the edges of the metal can lid so that you don't cut yourself.

2. Draw two lines across the lid in the form of a large + sign to divide the lid into four quarters.

3. Paint the quarters of the lid black and white so that the white and black are next to each other.

4. Using the hammer and nail, make a hole in the center of the lid.

5. Screw the eyebolt through the nut and then the washer, and then push the eyebolt through the hole in the lid.

6. Place the second washer and nut onto the eyebolt on the underside of the lid.

7. Tie your cord to the eyebolt and, using the ruler, make a knot in the cord at one-foot or one-meter intervals.

8. To use the disc, go out on a sunny day and lower it into the water from a dock or a boat.

9. Keep count of the number of knots that go into the water. Watch the black-and-white disc until in disappears from view. Record the depth at which this happens. Lower the disc farther and then raise it again until it just appears. Record the number of knots.

10. Add your two measurements together and divide by two. This number is the average. It tells you the depth to which light penetrates the water.

11. Try the procedure from a different place. What do you think would happen if you took a reading right after a storm that stirred up the water? What effect might water pollution have on the ability of light to penetrate the water? How might this affect the ocean food chain?

been passed along the food chain and is now stored in the fish. The bird will use the energy for growing, flying, and more fishing. It will lose some of its energy in the form of droppings and the heat it releases. Droppings contain nutrients that will be used in turn by the phytoplankton in the water or by bacteria if the waste is deposited on land.

In this story of energy, the phytoplankton is a **producer** because it uses energy from the sun to produce sugars that animals can use as food. The zooplankton is a plant eater, or **primary consumer**. The fish and bird are **secondary consumers** because they eat primary consumers. The bird is also considered a **predator** because it hunts and kills other organisms for food. Bacteria and other organisms that break down wastes and dead matter are called decomposers. The decomposed matter provides the nutrients needed by the phytoplankton to produce food. The producers, consumers, and decomposers all work together to cycle and recycle the energy in the food chain.

This is just one example of a food chain. Food chains are as numerous as the members of a biological community. Some begin with different producers such as eelgrass, kelp, or other marine algae. Many plants and animals are part of several different food chains. When the different food chains interconnect and overlap, they form a large network called a **food web**. Food chains and food webs may contain hundreds of different species of plants and animals, and they may span across many different habitats. Gulls for instance, one of the more familiar coastal residents, often belong to food chains that include the nearshore waters, the intertidal zone, and the land that stretches far beyond the shore.

The Pacific coast is a mosaic of habitats that are unified by the constant and ever-changing influence of the ocean. Except for the rhythmic pounding of the surf and the vast expanse of ocean behind it, many coastal communities seem to have few elements in common. In this book, we will examine some of these communities that make the Pacific coast their home and how together they create a unified ecosystem. We will explore Oregon's rocky intertidal zone, follow a salmon through the coastal waters of British Columbia, dive into a kelp forest in California, track an unusual seabird into the tops of coastal redwood trees, and follow the gray whale from Alaska to Mexico's

A familiar face at the seashore, the gull is a scavenger and an important part of many coastal food chains.

Baja Peninsula. We will also explore how people fit into this ecosystem. The Pacific coast is one of the most populous areas of North America and our impact on this ecosystem has caused many serious problems. But as we are learning about the fragile connections that hold ecosystems together, we are also learning how to protect them and ensure their future.

Holding On

With a force that could easily knock you off your feet, the waves crash against the coastline, pounding the solid jagged rock that juts out into the Pacific Ocean. This is Cape Arago, a rugged headland on the southern coast of Oregon. Many visitors to Cape Arago enjoy the view of this stunning rocky coastline from scenic overlooks well above the tossing waves. But not you. You scramble down onto the rocks for a close-up view of one of the Pacific coast's most diverse biological communities. Thanks to your good sense and tide chart, you've timed your visit to Cape Arago at low tide when much of the rock is exposed and you have plenty of time to explore before the water moves back in again. You know the rules: look with your eyes—not your hands, don't turn your back to the tide, and watch out for big waves.

At low tide, you have plenty of time to wander, to wonder, and to try and think like an ecologist. Ecologists spend a lot of time asking themselves questions. Some of the questions they might pose about the rocky coast are: How can anything live on a rock? How can they survive being battered by the waves? And what do these creatures do all day?

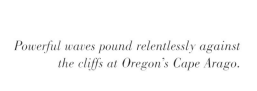

Powerful waves pound relentlessly against the cliffs at Oregon's Cape Arago.

Sea stars, mussels, and barnacles form a tight, yet competitive, community. They occupy the lowest intertidal zone, where they are able to survive brief periods of exposure to air and direct sunlight.

The first thing you notice about the rocks is that they are covered with matter that is small, low-lying, and firmly attached to the rock. You correctly assume these attachments are living things. Nothing sticks up more than a few inches and not a single organism is knocked off by the waves as they crash against the rocks. The only thing moving is the seaweed that swishes back and forth in the waves at the water's edge. You recognize only a few of the life-forms here— seaweed, black mussels, and some large orange sea stars (often called starfish). Other than that, the inhabitants are strange to you. And what is even stranger is that they are all grouped together in separate horizontal bands that extend across the entire face of the rock. You sit on a rock, puzzled. What is going on here?

Grab Hold, Stay Low

Your first impressions of the rocky coast hold some of the answers. To survive here plants and animals must be low lying and well attached. These are **adaptations**, or special features that help them survive in a particular environment. They must be low lying to reduce the impact of the waves that would otherwise easily dislodge them. Most animals are flat or just a few inches high. Some, such as the limpet and sea urchin, even dig into the rock, scraping out a depression with their filelike teeth called radula. Large algae such as the feather boa kelp can grow to 49 feet (15 m), but you will never see them sticking up out of the water. They lie flat, floating on the surface of the water.

Plants and animals of the rocky coast must also be well attached. The feather boa and other varieties of kelp have strong root-like structures called **holdfasts**, which anchor them to the rocks. These holdfasts don't move, but the upper parts of the plants are flexible, almost rubbery—an adaptation that helps the stems survive being tossed about by the waves without breaking. On a sandy beach, animals can burrow into the soft sand to protect themselves from the waves. But on the rocky coast, they must attach themselves to the rock. They cling to the rocks (and often to each other) with an amazing variety of suction cups, rootlike fibers, glue, and cement that are either part of their bodies or made by them. Barnacles are tiny crustaceans that glue their heads to the rock and build hard cone-shaped shelters around themselves, which they cement to the rock. The glue is so strong that scientists have been trying to manufacture a similar glue for dentists to use. Mussels fasten themselves with strong fibers called byssus, which are secreted by a gland near its fleshy foot. This makes mussels look as if they are rooted to the rock like plants.

These adaptations explain how the organisms attach themselves. But they don't explain why they attach themselves in particular places or why they are grouped into horizontal bands. Your tide chart holds some of the answers. Twice each day, the rocks at Cape Arago are covered and uncovered by the tides. Between the highest and the lowest points the water reaches is an area called the intertidal zone. Life-forms settle at certain points within this zone according to how long they can survive being exposed to the air during low tide and being submerged in water during high tides.

The spray zone (also called the splash zone) is the uppermost part of the rocky shore. The rocks here are almost always exposed to air, receiving only random spray from the waves. Patches of algae and lichen are abundant in this zone as are the tiny rock louse, an insect that breathes air and obtains its moisture by dipping its tail into pools of water trapped in the rocks. Certain kinds of snails called periwinkles and limpets live in this upper zone as well. The periwinkle grazes on algae and can survive out of water for two months. It retains moisture by closing its shell. The limpet, a snail with a tiny cone-shaped shell, lowers its shell tightly against the rock to avoid drying out.

Less harsh than the splash zone, the upper tidal zone is exposed twice a day by both of the low tides. Algae, such as rockweeds, are common here. These seaweeds have a gel-like substance within their blades to protect them from drying out. Many animals, such as turban snails and acorn barnacles, live beneath the damp masses of rock-weed where they are protected from the sun, drying air, and predators. Goose barnacles, sea anemones, and black mussels cannot survive exposure to the air for long, so they have settled in a band called the mid-intertidal zone, where they are exposed by the lower of the two daily tides. Below this zone is the low intertidal zone, which is exposed only during the lowest of the tides. Brown sea cabbage, sponges, sea stars, and sea urchins are abundant in this zone and can tolerate only the briefest exposure to the air.

Battles between the Tides

So far, you might have the impression that nothing is really happening in the intertidal community. Organisms are tightly attached, suitably located, and seem to be stationary. But there must be something else going on here, right? It may be difficult to imagine, but most of these seemingly passive organisms are involved in ongoing and often brutal battles. The struggle isn't over food as most of the animals filter plankton that is brought in regularly with the tides. Instead, the organisms here compete for the limited amount of space available within the intertidal zone. This combat involves stinging, crushing, undercutting, smothering, and raw animal power.

Take a look at the acorn barnacles. Different species of acorn barnacles are different sizes—from about $1/2$ inch to 5 inches (1.2 to 12 cm) wide. These different species live next to each other where they seem to be peacefully coexisting, but in truth they are slowly undercutting each other. The larger barnacles build more and more

Delicate and beautiful, this green anemone is also armed and dangerous. Stinging cells in its tentacles create a toxic boundary the smaller anemones do not cross.

layers on the outside of their shelter. As the shelter widens, its base, where the barnacle adheres to the surface of the rock, loosens and dislodges the smaller barnacles. These barnacles will most likely be knocked off by the next wave. Smaller barnacles may also be crushed in between two larger barnacles growing toward each other or smothered by a barnacle growing on top of it.

Some of the most intriguing battles fought in the intertidal community are between the sea anemones. These jellyfish cousins come in many different colors, but are usually a pale green. When opened, they expose a ring of delicate tentacles that sway gently in the water. Many species of anemones live in densely packed clusters and can reproduce by splitting themselves apart. As they move slowly around the rocks, some anemones may leave behind fragments of their body tissue. This tissue may grow into adult anemones. Other anemones pull themselves apart into two halves. Both methods result in genetically identical anemones called clones. The clones clump together, but when clones from one species bump into clones of a different species, that means war. The threatened clones fire toxic threads at one another from stinging capsules at the base of their beautiful tentacles. The injured clones retreat, leaving a narrow anemone-free strip between the clashing factions.

Mussels look like fairly harmless members of the intertidal community as well. With the sharp edges of their shells they passively shred the soft kelp trying to establish its holdfast in the same spot. By keeping the enemy out, the mussels ensure they have space to expand their population. New mussels take hold, and the older mussels can stage a gradual "takeover" by dissolving their byssus and producing new ones just a little farther away.

But they can only go so far, and their lower boundary is controlled not by a competitor, but by a predator—the ochre sea star, the terror of the mussel bed. This five-armed animal drapes or hunches itself over the mussel and latches onto it, pulling it apart with the tentacles on the underside of each arm. The mussel tries to stay shut, but if it opens slightly, the starfish extends its stomach out of its body and into the mussel to devour the soft body inside.

Please Disturb . . . A Little

Competition and predation in the intertidal community isn't all bad. Biologists call this kind of behavior where species are removed from their habitat disturbances. These disturbances increase the **biodiversity**, or number of different species, in the intertidal community. In removing organisms from the rocks, sea stars, mussels, barnacles, and anemones open up spaces for other organisms to move in. As sea stars eat their way through the mussel beds, they clear space for other animals and plants that could not penetrate the mussel beds on their own.

Other forces outside the intertidal community cause disturbances, too. Seabirds such as oyster catchers probe the exposed rocks for limpets and mussels. Winter storms on the Pacific coast bring powerful waves that bash the shore, wiping out entire mussel beds and tearing algae from its holdfasts. Driftwood can knock against the rocks crushing or loosening any organism it encounters. Along the rocky coast, nothing is completely safe from disturbances.

Too many disturbances, however, can have the opposite effect. Studies at Cape Arago and elsewhere have shown that the crushing footsteps of people visiting the intertidal zone can prevent many organisms from taking hold. Also, the uncontrolled harvesting of mussels creates large patches of bare rock that only barnacles can colonize before the next harvest. Other creatures living next to the mussels cannot move quickly enough to exploit the new territory. These kinds of disturbances cause harmful changes in the relationships between organisms and reduce the biodiversity of the intertidal community. When visiting the rocky coast, it is important for us to step lightly and let nature do the disturbing.

Although it appears to be resting on this mussel bed, the ochre sea star is actually devouring the soft insides of these small crustaceans. In its wake, the sea star will leave a strip of exposed, mussel-free rock, which is quickly occupied by a variety of less-aggressive organisms.

Making the Rounds

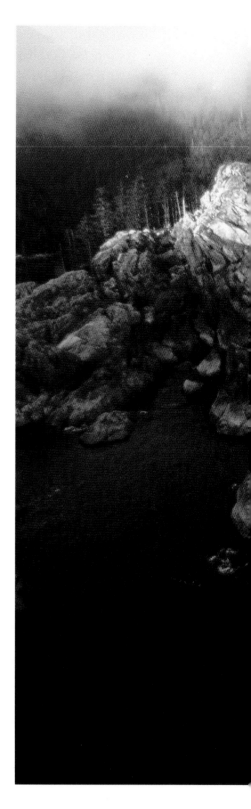

It is a rainy, blustery autumn day on Canada's Moresby Island, a remote and forested place about 62 miles (100 km) off the coast of British Columbia. Here you can kayak in the open ocean, explore an estuary, picnic by a stream, visit an old-growth forest, or watch bald eagles, black bears, seals, and sea lions. But how are you going to find all these things? By following one animal—the salmon. In different stages of its unusual life, this fish swims in the salty ocean, in the estuaries where the water is a mixture of both salty and fresh, and in the freshwater streams, such as the one that cross Moresby Island. The salmon relies on all of these habitats, and hundreds of animals in each habitat rely on the salmon. The salmon is the key to understanding the connections between very different habitats within the coastal ecosystem.

Follow the Salmon

Adult salmon live in the surface waters of the ocean feeding on fish such as anchovies, herrings, and young rockfish. In the late summer or fall, the adults begin their **migration**, or their annual seasonal journey from one place to another. Salmon are **anadromous**, that is,

Canada's South Moresby Island meets the needs of migrating salmon: a salty ocean, brackish estuaries, and freshwater streams.

they are fish that enter rivers from the sea and swim upstream to spawn, or lay their eggs. This means they are moving from a saltwater to a freshwater environment—a very drastic change for a fish. Even for the salmon, which have ways to regulate the amount of water and salt in their bodies, this change takes some getting used to.

The water in the estuary is **brackish**, or partly salty and partly fresh. This makes the estuaries a critical transition zone for the salmon. Usually in September, the adult ocean-going salmon begin congregating by the thousands in the estuaries of Moresby Island. They stop eating, and their bodies begin adjusting to the fresher water. After a few days, they begin swimming upstream, leaping up small waterfalls often twenty at a time. They usually travel only about 500 yards (457 m) upstream. In the gravelly riverbed, the female salmon thrashes her whole body to make several shallow hollows. In these nests she lays from 2,000 to 5,000 eggs. Then the male salmon swims

Driven by instinct, these migrating salmon leap up a waterfall as they swim toward their traditional spawning grounds—the freshwater stream of their birth.

over the nest and fertilizes the eggs. Shortly after spawning both male and female salmon die. The eggs hatch and the young fish live in the stream for a few years before returning to the estuary where their bodies make the transition to the salty ocean. Dense beds of eelgrass grow in the muddy sediments and shallow water of the estuary and provide the young salmon shelter from predators. The eelgrass, in turn, harbors many species of marine organisms, such as plankton and insects, which the salmon eat.

During their lives at sea, in estuaries, and in streams, salmon are important food for many animals. Larger fish, whales, eagles, seals, sea lions, and bears prey upon adult salmon. Other fish and birds eat the young salmon maturing in the streams and estuaries. Small fish, invertebrates in the streams, eat salmon eggs. Recently, biologists have discovered that salmon are even more important to coastal ecosystems *after* they spawn and die. Salmon bring a wealth of nutrients from the ocean into coastal streams and forests. When salmon die, their nutrient-filled bodies are consumed by a large and varied biological community, which includes everything from microscopic decomposers, more than twenty species of scavenging birds, and mammals such as the black bear.

Feast in the Forest

On Moresby Island, black bears gather along the stream banks and in rivers each fall to catch salmon swimming upstream and leaping up small waterfalls. This seasonal feast provides the bears with their major source of protein for the entire year. It also comes at a time when they need to gain extra weight so they can sleep through the winter. One biologist tracked 8 black bears during a 45-day-long spawning season and calculated that each bear ate about 13 salmon a day and in total consumed more than 4,500 salmon. That's a lot of fish—about 75 percent of the entire run—but it doesn't reduce the future salmon population. Most of the salmon eaten by the bears had already completed their spawning and were about to die. These weaker salmon may be easier to catch than the more robust ones that have not yet spawned. By eating mostly spawned salmon, the bears ensure themselves another salmon feast the next year.

Taking advantage of the fall salmon run, black bears eat only certain parts of the fish. They leave most of the carcass to other species of animals living in the stream and surrounding forest.

But bears are only the beginning of the salmon's afterlife. Bears rarely eat an entire salmon. They usually pull their catch onto the stream bank and into the forest, eat certain choice parts, and then abandon the carcass. This means leftovers for mammals such as otters, raccoons, skunks, weasel-like martens, and even white-tailed deer. Gulls, crows, ravens, wrens, shrews, mice, and other small creatures of the forest join these scavengers. Decomposers, such as beetles and flies, consume bits of salmon and carry the nutrients into the soil. The carcasses often remain on the stream banks and forest floor through the winter, sustaining many animals at a time when other food supplies are not available.

Many salmon carcasses stay in the stream where they are an

A Web of Nutrients

Herring
gull

Pine marten

Harbor seals

Crow

Black
bear

Black bear
with salmon

Salmon
in stream

Dead fish

Many creatures in forest and freshwater communities depend on the nutrients that migrating salmon bring from the ocean. The efficient recycling of energy is an important part of a healthy ecosystem.

important food source for the aquatic community. Algae, fungi, and bacteria growing on rocks in the stream act as sponges, taking in nutrients from the decaying salmon. Stream-dwelling insects scrape the rocks and consume these microscopic organisms. They also feed on tiny pieces of salmon, which they filter from the water or gather from the streambed. Hundreds of insects, such as caddis flies, may crowd together on a single salmon head. The salmon carcasses and the insects feeding on them are the key to the survival of the next generation of salmon. Young salmon emerge from their eggs in the early spring and spend nearly a year in their home streams. When the adults return in the fall, the young salmon feed heavily on their carcasses, the newly laid eggs, and the scavenging insects. One researcher found that with the arrival of the migrating adults, juvenile salmon doubled in size.

All levels of salmon consumers—the predators, the scavengers, and the decomposers—are part of a complex food web that stretches between the ocean and the coastal forests. Imagine a salmon as a package of nutrients or energy. During its life in the ocean, it consumes anchovies, herrings, young rockfish, and many other fish. These fish have eaten smaller fish, crustaceans, and perhaps squid. These animals dined on invertebrates and smaller fish that once fed on zooplankton. The zooplankton ate phytoplankton, which got their energy from the ultimate source—the sun. The salmon thus contains nutrients or energy derived from all of these sources. When it migrates, it takes these nutrients into an environment that lacks them—the freshwater stream. Here, the nutrients enrich the stream and make it a suitable habitat for more salmon. Without salmon carcasses there would be less algae and fewer stream-dwelling insects, fish, and forest animals that could survive through the winter.

Restoring the Salmon

On Moresby Island, the runs of migrating salmon are strong, relative to other parts of the coast. The streams are healthy, the estuaries are full of life, and wildlife is abundant in the forests. Elsewhere on the Pacific coast, however, salmon runs are becoming less common and have disappeared entirely in many rivers and streams where they were once abundant. Sadly, these rivers and streams aren't like the ones on Moresby Island. Many of them have been polluted and dammed. Estuaries have been filled with sediment and pollutants. The forests the rivers flow through have been cut down. Homes, highways, farms, factories, and shipping ports have destroyed much of the habitat needed by the salmon. And the salmon population has been reduced drastically over the last decade by overharvesting by commercial fishing.

In many areas, people are trying to restore salmon runs. In the United States, Alaska, Washington, Oregon, and California were granted $50 million in federal funds to support salmon recovery programs. But this doesn't mean simply replenishing streams with farm-raised salmon. It means restoring the salmon's habitats by cleaning up polluted rivers, protecting estuaries, replanting forests, and removing or opening dams that block migrating fish from reaching their spawning sites. It also means raising public awareness about the plight of the salmon and encouraging those living on the Pacific coast and beyond to help in the restoration efforts.

Biologists track salmon with the aid of high-tech scanners and with microchips implanted directly in the fish. Monitoring salmon may help scientists understand the recent decline in salmon runs in the Pacific's coastal streams and rivers.

The Underwater Forest

You can understand and enjoy many of the coastal communities from the dry side of the coast. But to explore the undersea forests of California's Monterey Bay, you'll need to get on and in the water. But not in your bathing suit. Even in summer the ocean here can be as cold as a glass of ice water. A kayak, a wet suit, and scuba or snorkeling gear will be necessary. Luckily, these are easy to rent in the town on the bay. In less than an hour you've outfitted yourself and found an ecologist guide to lead the way.

And you'll need a guide. The undersea world you are visiting is part of the Monterey Bay National Marine Sanctuary—a preserve about the size of Connecticut. It runs 350 miles (563 km) along the California coast, extending from the high-tide mark onshore to as far as 57 miles (91 km) offshore. It is the largest marine sanctuary in the world after Australia's Great Barrier Reef. You wouldn't want to get lost.

Creating a Community

From the rocky coast, you step into your kayak and push off into the bay. The water is calm. You are in the **subtidal zone**, or the area of the coastal waters that is

Beyond the rocky shore and beneath the surging waves of California's Monterey Bay lies the hidden world of the kelp forest.

not exposed by low tides. There are no breaking waves, just the gentle rising and falling of the water. Your paddle keeps getting tangled in the mat of slimy rubbery brown seaweed on the surface of the water. This is giant kelp, an alga that can grow up to 100 feet (30 m) long at a rate of 18 inches (46 cm) a day. Giant kelp is the main producer in the subtidal food chain. It spreads its huge leaflike blades out along the water's surface to collect sunlight. From these blades, the kelp's **stipe**, or thick stem, leads down to the rocky bottom of the bay where it attaches itself by its holdfast. These plants are strong, and their effect on your paddling technique is noticeable.

Sunlight penetrates the water and illuminates the forest of giant kelp—an algae that houses and feeds thousands of different plants and animals.

The kelp also has a large effect on its community. It is the main habitat-forming species in the bay. Its blades, stipes, and holdfasts provide food, shelter, and living space for as many as 1,000 species of marine plants and animals. One of them is watching you untangle your paddle from the kelp.

It is a sea otter floating on its back. It looks tangled in the kelp, too. Actually, these furry mammals wrap fronds of kelp around themselves and their young pups on purpose to keep from floating away while they sleep. Sea otters live year-round in the cold waters of Monterey Bay. Unlike many other sea mammals such as seals or sea lions, sea otters do not have a thick layer of blubber to keep them warm. Instead, they have incredibly thick fur—the densest of any marine mammal. Sea otter coats have up to a million hairs per square inch (about 156,000 per sq. cm). By comparison, humans have an average total of about 20,000 hairs on their heads. This fur traps layers of air, which act as insulation. Sea otters spend much of their time grooming their fur, especially the long outer hairs that guard their dense underfur. In order for their coats to be waterproof, these

Sea otters feast on sea stars and an enormous variety of marine animals they collect from the kelp forest floor. The otter eats and rests on its back, often supported by a floating bed of kelp blades.

hairs must be absolutely clean. If the hairs are dirty or stuck together in clumps, the underfur gets wet and the animal becomes too chilled and dies.

But clean fur alone won't keep sea otters warm. They must also eat a huge amount of food each day. A single adult weighing about 65 pounds (29.5 kg) eats about 20 pounds (9 kg) of food a day to nourish it and keep it warm. So when they are not grooming their coats, sea otters spend a lot of time diving down into the kelp forest to find food. With your wet suit and scuba gear, you can join the sea otter in the kelp forest.

A Swim in the Forest

You slip into the water, down through the canopy, or top layer, of golden-brown kelp. You swim between the long stipes, which grow straight up from the bottom like columns. The dense canopy filters out much of the light, but shafts of sun filter down through the gently swaying underwater forest.

Many of the animals in this underwater realm hold on or attach themselves to the kelp to keep from being washed out to sea or onto shore. Clinging to the stipes with their suction cup-like bodies, you'll see purple-colored top snails, black limpets, and white turban snails. While they act like consumers, they don't have the kind of teeth needed to pierce healthy kelp. With their rasping filelike teeth called radulae, they graze on the tiny algae growing on the kelp. If you stare at the kelp long enough, you'll also see kelp crabs feeding there. These small crustaceans match the kelp's color and semi-transparent quality almost exactly. These crabs begin their lives among the plankton, then move to the lower intertidal zone to mature. When they are big enough, they migrate to the kelp forest where their camouflaging coloration helps them hide from sea otters and other predators.

Fish are abundant in the kelp forest, seeking shelter and food among the stipes. They are mostly secondary consumers since their diet consists of other animals. Blue-and-red-striped blennies feed on small invertebrates, plankton, and other bits of food floating in the forest. Senioritas are long thin fish that are the "cleaners" of the kelp. They pick parasites off other fish and eat the small snails and crustaceans living on the stipes. Many fish have names that show their close connection to the kelp forest: kelp bass, kelp rockfish, and giant kelpfish. Though they are different sizes and shapes, they closely match the kelp in color and, like the kelp crab, are well camouflaged as they swim through the kelp looking for each other and for crustaceans, squid, octopus, and other invertebrates to eat. Many kinds of fish live beyond the kelp bed as adults, but use the kelp forest as a fish hatchery and nursery. They lay their eggs here and the young fish mature in between kelp fronds before heading out to sea themselves.

As you drift down through the kelp forest you find yourself on the bay's rocky bottom. Among the rocks and a network of kelp holdfasts are the homes of many animals including sea stars, crabs, scallops, abalone, and sea urchins. The purple sea urchins use their teeth and spines to excavate pits in the rock where they find shelter

Red sea urchins—a favorite food of sea otters—normally graze on the algae that grows on rocks. Without the otters, the uncontrolled population of urchins would deplete this food supply and begin to overgraze the kelp beds.

from the waves. Urchins are primary consumers that feed on drifting algae. From a distance you watch a sea otter hunting among the rocks. It picks up a small rock and uses it to dislodge an sea urchin—a meal that looks rather unappetizing. But protected by the sharp spines is the soft and edible body of the urchin—one of the sea otter's favorite foods. With a few urchins in hand, the sea otter swims back to the surface of the water to dine in the canopy. Using its chest as a kind of lunch counter, it carefully bites through the urchin spines to get at the sweet urchin meat inside.

Urchin Barrens

What you've just watched is a simple act: a sea otter eating an urchin—a predator eating its prey. The sea otter benefits directly from the nourishment the urchin provides. But this simple act is more complex than that. The sea otter and the urchin have a predator-prey relationship that has developed over many thousands, even millions of years. The sea urchins feed by scraping algae off the rocks. If there are too many urchins, they deplete the algae on the rocks and begin eating the kelp. As they scrape at the base of the kelp stipe, they chew through it, causing it to detach from its holdfast and float away. Once this kelp is gone the urchins begin to die off. By eating urchins, the sea otters ensure that the urchin population has enough to eat and a habitat to eat it in. As in all predator-prey relationships, the predator benefits directly (otters get energy from eating urchins), and the prey benefits indirectly (the urchins can sustain a healthy population). The kelp itself and other members of the kelp forest benefit indirectly, too. The otters prevent the urchins from overharvesting the kelp. A healthy kelp forest provides homes and a feeding ground for many organisms whose wastes nourish not only the kelp but also some algae that the urchins scrape off the rocks.

Two hundred years ago, the sea otter population in California was about 16,000. By the end of the 1800s, fur hunters had reduced the population to about thirty otters living just south of Monterey Bay. With so few otters, the sea urchin population exploded. Entire kelp plants, representing food and habitat for hundreds of animals, were detached at the base and carried away by the surf. Without the dense beds of kelp, members of the community floated out to see on the blades, moved elsewhere, or were easily discovered and eaten by their predators. The once lush shady underwater forest became more like a desert—a sunlit ocean bottom where instead of cactuses, only spiny urchins lived. The sea otters moved away as well: though there was a banquet of urchins to feast on, there was no kelp for the otters to float on or wrap themselves in while they slept.

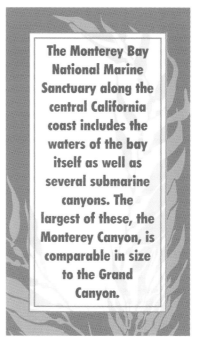

The Monterey Bay National Marine Sanctuary along the central California coast includes the waters of the bay itself as well as several submarine canyons. The largest of these, the Monterey Canyon, is comparable in size to the Grand Canyon.

Without the kelp to eat, the urchins began to starve and die. The urchin population declined and slowly, on the sunlit bottom of the bay, the kelp began to reestablish a foothold. But as soon as it did, the remaining urchins devoured the new plants as well. Without the sea otters to keep the urchins in check, the kelp didn't stand a chance of growing large and dense enough to create a forest. And without a kelp forest, the community didn't stand a chance or being reunited. The sea otters were critical to the recovery and balance of the entire kelp community. In many ecosystems, the loss of just one species upsets the entire balance between the thousands of other species that make up that ecosystem.

In the early twentieth century, laws were passed to make it illegal to kill a sea otter or sell its pelt. Special refuges and marine sanctuaries were established along the California coast to further protect these animals and their habitat. Sea otters have responded to these protections, but very slowly. There are now about two thousand sea otters along the California coast—a small fraction of their original population. Within the Monterey Bay National Marine Sanctuary, there are areas where the sea otters can live in a balanced relationship with the urchins. These are places where the kelp forests are lush and healthy. Recovered and protected, the sanctuary also offers places for people to come and observe the interaction of these diverse, yet fascinating, organisms.

A Species in Check

It is a late summer afternoon on California's northern coast. You are out for a stroll on the narrow sandy beach in Prairie Creek Redwoods State Park to watch the sun set over the Pacific Ocean. You've spread out your blanket and brought your sunglasses, binoculars, and a sweater. Though it is summer, the cool water and ocean breezes keep the climate moderate most of the year. Waves break and roll over large offshore rocks where dozens of seabirds are nesting. The gulls, cormorants, murres, and auklets fly and swoop over the shore, snatching fish from the sea, and trying to keep their perch on the steep rocks. You take out your binoculars to get a closer view, but a blanket of fog appears and begins to spread across the water toward you. Fog is a daily event along the coast where warm inland air moves over the cold Pacific water and condenses. You pack up your things, put away your sunglasses, and decide to move on.

You turn your back to the ocean and the birds and walk along a trail toward the forest of evergreen trees that seem to spill down the cliffs and into the sea. You enter the forest and, after a few moments, come upon a small group of people with binoculars staring up into an enormous tree. You are curious and decide to

The rocky cliffs of the California coast host thousands of nesting seabirds, such as cormorants, gulls, and pelicans.

ask (in a whisper) what they are doing. No one speaks. One person scribbles something in her notebook and hands it to you. It says "marbled murrelet."

At the time, you had no idea what these two words meant. But your curiosity got the best of you and in the weeks following your encounter, you learned that a marbled murrelet is a seabird. It is about the size of a robin, has a thick neck, webbed feet, and plumage that is mostly brown with patches of marbled black and white on its belly. Like most seabirds, it spends much of its life in the open ocean and coastal waters catching fish. But unlike most seabirds that nest on offshore rocks and cliffs, marbled murrelets nest in coastal forests. But not just any coastal forest. In California, the murrelets prefer old-growth forests or mature forests where trees are at least 180 years old and at least 200 feet (60 m) tall. The trees that meet these requirements are often Douglas fir, western hemlock, sitka spruce, and at Prairie Creek, coast redwoods—the world's tallest living things. It is in the middle of the crown of these impressive giants that the marbled murrelet lays its egg.

For centuries scientists suspected that the murrelets nested in the ancient coastal forests, but no one had ever found a nest with a murrelet in it until 1974. This is quite late in the world of ornithology, or the study of birds, since the nests of nearly all 800 known North American bird species had already been documented long before this. The discovery of the nest was made accidentally by a tree trimmer removing storm-weakened branches in an old-growth forest. Since then, forest ecologists, marine biologists, ornithologists, and others from the scientific community as well as amateur birders have turned their attention to this unusual seabird. What they have learned about the murrelet's nesting behavior is fascinating. But even more intriguing are the secrets the murrelets have revealed about the connections between very different habitats within the coastal ecosystem.

Tracking the Murrelet

Before the discovery of the nest in 1974, scientists knew a lot about marbled murrelets from observing them on the ocean. They knew that during the fall and winter murrelets spend most of their time fishing

The murrelet lays its egg in the moss and lichen found in the crowns of towering redwoods, Douglas firs, and other old-growth trees.

underwater for herring, anchovies, perch, sardines, and rockfish in coastal waters. In the springtime, they move closer to the shore to find mates. After a dancelike courtship on the water, the mated pair flies into the forest where they are rarely seen again. Scientists could only guess that they spend the summer flying to and from their nest feeding their chicks fish from the ocean.

What took scientists so long to locate a nest? In the forest, the murrelet's dark plumage camouflages it against the tree trunks. Marbled murrelets are **crepuscular**, that is, active around dawn and dusk—a time of dim light and usually lots of fog here on the northern Pacific coast. Also murrelets are incredibly strong flyers. Radar has measured speeds up to 60 miles per hour (96.5 km/h), making them even more difficult to detect. A murrelet nest, one would think, would be easier to find. But these birds don't actually build nests. They use the natural cushions of moss and lichen growing on wide branches near the tops of the towering redwoods. So imagine climbing to the top of a redwood tree to search each and every clump of moss for a tiny egg or a chick. The easier-to-spot adults would have flown out of the nest as soon as they detected a large creature with binoculars moving toward them. The search would be futile.

It comes as no surprise then that by 1984, scientists had only discovered one more nest on the Pacific coast—on the shoreline of Alaska. People were getting worried. They needed to find more murrelet nests in California, Oregon, and Washington State. And they needed to find them quickly. Why the rush? In choosing the coastal redwood for its nesting site, the marbled murrelet also chose the very same tree valued by people for its beautiful and durable wood.

Since the 1850s, approximately 96 percent of the old-growth coast redwoods have been harvested for homes, decks, boats, and furniture. The remaining trees grow in a narrow band along the coast. In California less than half of the ancient redwood forests are protected in parks. The rest are owned privately, mostly by timber companies that are actively logging the trees. Growing numbers of people became worried that the marbled murrelet will become extinct if the logging of redwoods wasn't stopped or controlled. They had to prove that the murrelet depended on ancient forests of coast redwoods for its survival. But four murrelet nests weren't enough to prove this. No timber company would give up cutting down a redwood worth $100,000 for a few murrelets that might not actually live in that tree.

Scientists had to overcome many challenges and work creatively to find more murrelet nests. They did much of their work in the forests before dawn, tracking birds by sight and by hearing their calls. They searched on their hands and knees on the forest floor to find chicks that had fallen out of their nests. Those who were trained and equipped to climb ropes hoisted themselves up into the treetops to search for nests. They set up automatic video cameras and special photographic equipment to catch the birds on film. Over the months and years of research, scientists found many more nests that helped them piece together clues to the murrelet's relationship to the coast redwoods.

Steller's jays and other birds prey on murrelet nests during both the egg and nestling stages.

Coastal Giants

The ancient coast redwoods are the required height and branch width for keeping the murrelets safest from their predators, which include Steller's jays, red-shouldered hawks, and flying squirrels. These predators plunder the nests in search of both eggs and chicks. These raids have a great impact on the murrelet population. Unlike other birds that lay several eggs each year, the murrelet lays only one egg per year. The loss of an egg reduces the murrelets' chance to add to their population.

The coast redwood of California is one of the few trees of its dimensions to grow in forests close to the Pacific Ocean. This is important to the murrelet since it gets its food from the ocean. Coast redwoods also grow farther inland, but they reach the greatest heights along the coast where the climate is cool, moist, and foggy. Coastal fog plays an important role in the lives of the redwoods, especially in the droughtlike California summer. The fog can add as much as 12 inches (30 cm) to the total amount of precipitation the trees receive each year. It also helps prevent the trees from drying out and becoming

It is often hard to see the entire length of a coast redwood. In addition to their great height, blanketing fog can create poor visibility. It also helps conceal the marbled murrelets and allows them to avoid detection from predators.

more likely to succumb to fire. The coastal environment, therefore, allows the redwoods to live longer (as much as 2,000 years) and grow to heights preferred by the murrelets. Their elevated homes keep them as far away from their predators as possible.

How much old-growth forest does a murrelet need? Can't it nest in a single redwood surrounded by other kinds of trees? These questions may be the most challenging for scientists to answer. Many people think that the 40,000 acres (16,200 ha) of old-growth redwoods preserved within Prairie Creek and other state and national parks are enough. But these parks do not form a solid redwood forest. They are a patchwork of different forests separated by highways, towns, and commercial timberlands that are open to logging. As the patches of forest are logged, the murrelet's habitat becomes further fragmented. This

habitat fragmentation will leave the murrelets more exposed to their predators living at the edge of the forest. Scientists are working to determine the minimum amount of unfragmented forest the murrelets need to survive.

But can't the murrelets move to another habitat in order to survive? No. Over millions of years, each species develops adaptations to survive in a specific habitat. A murrelet cannot simply "move next door" to a spruce forest or a younger stand when its nesting tree is cut down by power saws. Murrelets don't have the instincts to move to another habitat, or in some cases, even to a new stand of trees in the same forest. Once they've found a suitable home, generations of murrelets return to the same tree over and over again.

Saving the Murrelet

In 1992, after much delay, the marbled murrelet was declared a threatened species in Oregon, Washington State, and California. This means that its population is declining rapidly because of human impact. In California, it is also listed as an endangered species, a more serious status that means its population is declining to such low levels that, without help, it will become extinct. Marbled murrelet recovery teams are working with forestry experts and lumber companies to figure out a way to balance the human demand for redwood lumber with the murrelets' unspoken need to live in old-growth coast redwood forests. Logging projects in all three Pacific coast states have been delayed or stopped because of the presence of murrelets.

Today, one coast redwood is worth about $100,000. No one has put a price on marbled murrelets, and it is unlikely that most people will even notice if they disappear. But we cannot hold this view of the murrelet, or any other species—endangered, threatened, or abundant—if we want to be part of a living planet. As we allow species to disappear, we are unlinking food chains, reducing biodiversity, and paving the way for our own disappearance as a species. We need the murrelets to keep our ecosystems intact and for what they can teach us about the way our ecosystems work. Will we have time to learn the secrets the murrelets hold? Will we save our ancient forests before it is too late to learn from them?

Mammals on the Move

*Y*ou saw them in the distance from the shores of Gwaii Hanaas. Groups of schoolchildren saw them when they looked up from the tide pools of Cape Arago. Bird-watchers spotted them through their binoculars on the redwood coast. Kayakers in Monterey Bay got a glimpse of their backs and tails as they rose up from the sea. They are gray whales—more than 6,000 of them—migrating, or making a seasonal journey 6,000 miles (9,654 km) from Alaska to Mexico's Baja Peninsula. They follow the Pacific coast closely on their way south, often coming with 100 yards (90 m) of the shore.

Whale-watching is a popular activity along the Pacific coast. From land or by boat, everyone hopes to witness the spectacle of a 50-foot-long (15-m) gray whale breaching, or leaping straight out of the water and falling back with a huge splash. This is one of nature's greatest shows. But it only lasts a moment. Then the whale is gone, far beyond the range of our binoculars.

The whales do not make their long and arduous journey to entertain us. They migrate in order to survive. Gray whales rely on two very different coastal

Breaching gray whales are one of the Pacific coast's greatest natural spectacles. Each year whales migrate from Alaska to Mexico and back, traveling a distance unmatched by any mammal.

habitats for their survival needs: the cold, nutrient-rich waters of the Bering and Chukchi Seas off the Alaskan coast, and the warm birthing grounds along the Mexican coast. The seas supply food—tiny creatures called amphipods and tube worms that live in the sediments on the ocean floor. The shallow lagoons of the Baja Peninsula provide a protected place for the whales to bear their calves. Like all living things, gray whales need food and shelter, but for the whales, these basic needs are separated by thousands of miles. Their food is not found in Mexico, and there are no lagoons on the Alaskan coast. So the only way for gray whales to meet their survival needs is to migrate. Many mammals, such as bats, caribou, walruses, humpback whales, and fur seals, also make seasonal migrations for food and shelter, but the gray whales make the longest trek of all. Let's travel with them and find out why they travel such extreme distances to find just the right coastal habitats.

In 1857, Captain Charles Scammon discovered a lagoon in Baja California where the gray whales went to calve. This discovery brought whale hunters by the boatload and caused the gray whale population to drop from about 15,000 to 2,000 in just over 10 years.

Going to Extremes

Gray whales spend the late spring and summer in the icy-cold waters off the western coast of Alaska. There, the whales' main foods, amphipods and tube worms, are found in abundance on the ocean floor. Tens of thousands of these organisms can be found in a patch the size of a doormat. To consume these animals, the gray whale dives to within a few inches of the bottom of the ocean and sucks sediment and water into its mouth as it swims slowly forward. When its mouth is full, it expels the sediment and water through comblike plates, called baleen, in its upper jaw. It swallows what is left. After a few months of feeding on these tiny creatures, a gray whale can gain an additional 25 percent of its normal body weight. That's a lot of food for a whale weighing 30 to 40 tons (27,700 to 36,300 kg).

By early October, the gray whales have depleted their food supply. The pregnant females need a warm habitat to give birth to their calves, which are born without blubber to insulate and keep them warm in the frigid northern waters. They also need a place where they can protect

Gray whales are easy to spot as they travel in groups close to the shore. They breathe through their blowholes for a few minutes, then raise their flukes and submerge for several minutes to feed or swim.

their young from predators such as killer whales. The icy open Bering Sea is not the place. So the whales begin their long migration.

They swim southward toward Mexico at an average of 78 miles (125 km) a day. They stop to rest, but rarely to eat. They have spent the summer eating and can live off the body fat stored in their thick layer of blubber until they return to their feeding grounds the following spring. Scientists aren't sure why the whales don't feed, but they think that it might be too time consuming for the whales and thus delay their progress to the southern peninsula. If the pregnant females were to give birth in colder, northern water, it is most likely the calves would not survive. Amphipods and tube worms do live in the sediments along the coast farther south, but they occur in smaller patches in scattered locations. These locations are often in estuaries where the nutrient-rich sediments support larger populations of these tiny creatures. Occasionally, the whales will come into the estuaries to feed.

The journey to Mexico takes two to three months. By mid-February, almost all of the whales have reached the Baja Peninsula, a desertlike land of mountains, salt flats, and lagoons. These lagoons

Gray whales are considered friendly and frequently approach whale-watching boats that ply the nearshore waters. Kissing these fellow mammals is a rare opportunity.

are the gray whales' traditional calving grounds, the area where they return each year to bear their young. One of their favorite places is the warm waters of Laguna San Ignacio. The entrance to Laguna San Ignacio is protected by a sandbar, which shields the whales from heavy waves, sharks, and other predators waiting in the open water outside the lagoon.

In Laguna San Ignacio and several other lagoons, the females give birth to their calves during the late winter. A newborn calf measures about 15 feet (4.5 m) long and weighs up to 1,500 pounds (680 kg). The shallow water makes it easier for the mothers to keep track of their calves and easier for the calves to learn the proper breathing and diving rhythms. In the same way, many human children learn how to swim and blow bubbles in shallow wading pools. The mothers nurse their calves on milk that is 54 percent fat (about the consistency of soft butter). After two or three months of drinking about 10 gallons (38 l) of milk a day, the calves are strong enough and have put on enough weight to make the long journey north.

During their winter in Baja, gray whales also breed in the lagoons. Many of the northbound female whales leave the lagoon pregnant. They have just enough time—twelve to thirteen months—to migrate back to Alaska, feed for a few months, then travel back to Baja to give birth. By late spring, all the whales—mothers, calves, pregnant females, juveniles, and adult males—leave the lagoons and head north again along the coast. When they reach their feeding grounds, the sediments are again full of amphipods and tube worms for them to feast on.

The precise timing of the stages of a gray whale's life is mind boggling. They mate, gestate, give birth, nurse, feed, and store just the right amount of blubber to migrate great distances and take advantage of different habitats. Or is it the other way around? Ages ago, did the first gray whales migrate because they somehow learned that their chances of survival were greater if they gave birth and nurtured their young in Baja? No marine mammal expert or paleontologist studying whale fossils can fully answer these questions. The relationship between the gray whales, their food supply, their predators, and their distant coastal habitats has evolved over tens of thousands of year. When and why the first gray whales migrated is a mystery locked in the past.

> The gray whale is named for its blotchy gray color pattern. Some of this pattern is present at birth, but most of it is caused by barnacles growing in the skin or by depigmented areas where barnacles have been.

Population Puzzles

Gray whales were hunted to near extinction in the 1850s. They were easy prey because they came close to the shore, weren't afraid of boats and humans, and congregated in large numbers in shallow lagoons. In the 1940s, laws were passed to prohibit the killing of gray whales. Since then, their numbers have increased by about five hundred whales a year. By 1983, the population had almost reached the original total of 16,000. And today, with a population of about 20,000, gray whales remain an abiding symbol of the Pacific coast.

This is good news, but scientists are noticing some puzzling behavior. In 1998, the whale migration from the Bering Sea started very late. Researchers reported that the gray whales, which usually pass the central Oregon coast no later than December 10 every year, did not show up for three more weeks. And in May 1999, at least sixty-five dead gray whales washed ashore on the Baja Peninsula. This is the highest number of fatalities in the twenty-four years people have been tracking the whale migration.

These events are troubling scientists. They have no explanations for the late migration or deaths nor do they know if the two events are even related. But there are many theories that scientists are testing. Some theories relate these events to water pollution. Others focus on the unusual 1998–1999 El Niño weather patterns. The most likely theory, however, points to changes in the food supply in the whales' summer feeding grounds off Alaska.

Scientists are currently examining the Bering Sea to determine if the population of amphipods and tube worms has been depleted and why. Could commercial fishing be causing changes in the marine food chain that includes the amphipods and tube worms? The gray whale population, now 4,000 over its original number, grows by about 500 whales each year. Perhaps the whales have reached a natural peak in their population and the deaths are part of the natural process of population control. Perhaps the gray whales periodically deplete their food supply, die off in great numbers, then recover when their food supply has also revived. It will take time and the efforts of scientists all along the Pacific coast to find the answers.

Scientists inspect a beached gray whale to discover the cause of its death. Oil spills, depletion of their food supply, and changes in their habitats are the major threats to the gray whale's survival.

Blubber Gloves

The gray whales of the Pacific coast spend much of their lives in water as cold as 40 degrees Fahrenheit (about 4° Celsius). How do these warm-blooded mammals manage to stay warm? They have a thick layer of fat called blubber just beneath their skin. This activity lets you see how well blubber works.

You will need:

- three plastic bags (produce bags from the grocery store work well)
- a can of shortening (such as Crisco, which is similar to blubber)
- a plastic bucket of cold water
- a few trays of ice cubes
- a watch with a second hand

1. Fill a large bucket with cold water and ice cubes. The water should be cold enough so that the ice cubes do not melt instantly—similar to the water whales swim in.

2. Place your hand in the first plastic bag, gathering and holding the top of the bag closely around your forearm with your other hand. Place your hand in the bucket of ice water up to your wrist. Record how long you can keep your hand in the water. Note: Stop when it becomes uncomfortable—this is not an endurance test.

3. Take your hand out of the bag. Fill the second bag with the shortening (the easiest way to do this is to put your hand into the bag, scoop the shortening out with your hand, then turn the bag inside out).

4. Place your hand in the third plastic bag and then into the bag containing the shortening. With your free hand, mold the shortening around your hand in a somewhat even layer. You have just made half a pair of blubber gloves.

5. Place your blubber-gloved hand in the bucket of ice water. How does it feel compared to the first time you put your hand in the water? How does it feel after 30 seconds? After 1 minute? The blubber acts as insulation to keep your hand warm. In much greater quantities it helps whales maintain their body heat while they are swimming in icy water.

5. Did you also notice that the blubber kept your hand afloat in the water? Blubber is less dense than water so it floats on top of water. The buoyant blubber also helps keep the whales afloat.

Tomorrow's Pacific Coast

The Pacific coast ecosystem is always changing. Many of these changes have occurred naturally as the sea and the land meet and interact. The landforms, tidal rhythms, and wave patterns we see today are the result of billions of years of change. Plants and animals have evolved new forms and behaviors, and developed new communities in response to this dynamic environment. Some transformations have been slow, others more dramatic and sudden. In the last few hundred years, people have brought the most sudden alterations to the Pacific coast ecosystem. And because of the location of the coast, the changes are coming from both the land and the water.

With water comes the possibility of life. But when water is polluted, the potential diminishes. While the ocean looks beautiful and we enjoy swimming in it, it is not clean enough for many species of plants and animals to survive. Oil spills are one of the greatest and most constant threats to the coastal environment. Much of the oil that becomes fuel for our cars is pumped up from beneath the continental shelf. Oil derricks, platforms, and pumping rigs are scattered along much of the coast from Alaska to Mexico. Oil tankers ply the

The threat of oil spills looms large in Pacific coast ecosystems. The shipping lanes used by large tankers make a potentially hazardous playground for all marine species, especially these unsuspecting seals.

nearshore waters from Alaska to Mexico, bringing billions of gallons of oil into coastal ports from our own continent and oil-producing countries abroad. Accidental oil spills from these vessels have occurred too frequently and with devastating effects. Thick black oil sludge clogs the gills of fish and covers the coats of birds, marine mammals, and land animals as it washes ashore. As a result of the 1989 oil spill of the *Exxon Valdez* off the coast of Alaska, more than 300,000 birds, 2,600 sea otters, and tens of thousands of other animals were killed. The beaches of Prince William Sound still offer up oil residue from the spill, and recovery teams are still working to restore the environment more than ten years after the accident. In 1999, an oil tanker spilled 2000 gallons (7,570 l) in California's Humboldt Bay. More than six hundred oil-covered birds were rescued and some three hundred marine birds were killed, including fifteen marbled murrelets. From disasters like these, more than 100 million gallons (378 million l) of oil are spilled worldwide each year.

Water pollution also comes from the land, from the rivers that flow into the Pacific from thousands of miles away. And it is carried by the currents and the waves from all across the globe. Our coastal waters have become the dumping grounds for more than a century.

Despite human efforts to rescue oil-covered birds after a spill, most seabirds, such as this western grebe, stand little chance of survival. Many birds ingest the toxic oil as they clean their wings or die from exposure to cold water and air.

Sewage, chemical pollutants, garbage, hazardous wastes, and pesticides and herbicides that run off our land enter the ocean directly or through rivers and streams that flow into the Pacific. Contrary to what most people think, individuals—not industry—are the biggest culprits when it comes to ocean pollution. Most ocean pollution is caused by contaminated runoff from yards, parking lots, and roads.

Many of the animals that make the Pacific coast their home are threatened or endangered species. We have hunted sea otters to near extinction, destroyed much of the habitat of the marbled murrelet, and polluted the estuaries and dammed the coastal rivers where salmon migrate. Recovery teams are working to restore populations of these animals by protecting them and their habitats. But this will take many years. As we have seen with the sea otter, it is not enough to protect the animal itself. Their habitats and environments must be protected, too. Scientists were encouraged by the comeback of the sea otters, but as the number of otters slowly increases, so do its problems. Sea otters and fishermen are after the same quarry: abalone. A group of sea otters can quickly eat through a large area of abalone, leaving the fishermen nothing to harvest. To balance the needs of the sea otters, the fishermen, and the coastal ecosystem, wildlife biologists set up a "no-otter zone" along the coast of California where fishermen could harvest abalone. But this proved a difficult undertaking as finding and capturing the sea otters is time consuming and expensive. Maintaining the no-otter zone in 1992 cost nearly $10,000 per otter captured.

But there is hope that these efforts will work. Thanks to the hunting ban on gray whales, these animals have recently been taken off the threatened species list. But how long will they stay off? Gray whales are still being hunted in Alaska, Siberia, and now in Washington State where the Makah Indian tribe has a permit from the United States government to resume their ancient whale-hunting tradition. They have

California's first inhabitants were the Indians who lived along the coast as early as 10,000 B.C. The ancient people fished the coastal streams, estuaries, and nearshore waters, collected shellfish, and hunted marine mammals with little effect on the natural balance of the coastal ecosystems.

Some Native American tribes are allowed to hunt gray whales as part of their ancient traditions. Though the hunting is limited and carefully controlled, the practice is controversial and opposed by many conservation groups.

been allowed to kill up to five whales a year from 1998 to 2002.

Even if you do not live near the Pacific coast, hunt whales, eat abalone, or use redwood lumber, you are part of its ecosystem. Have you ever ridden in a car? It is likely that your gasoline comes from oil off the Pacific coast. Have you ever eaten ice cream? Used bottled salad dressing or toothpaste? If the answer is yes, you are a primary consumer in the kelp forest community. These products (and hundreds of others) contain algin, a substance found in kelp that is used to make many of the foods we eat smooth and creamy. Kelp is also rich in minerals and is an ingredient in vitamins for people, food for pets, and fertilizers for gardens. In the Monterey Bay National Marine Sanctuary and elsewhere along the California coast, tons of kelp are harvested commercially each year.

Harvesters are only allowed to cut the kelp 4 feet (1.2 m) below the surface, which many people claim doesn't damage the kelp forest. It may actually help the forest by allowing more light to reach younger kelp plants below the surface. But many others disagree. Even though the kelp grows back quickly, often in a few weeks, the destruction of the canopy displaces many of the animals that live there. Harvesting that isn't carefully regulated may begin to cause small breaks in the links that hold the kelp forest community together.

Who decides how much kelp is too much? How many gray whales are necessary or desirable? How much money and time should be spent on saving marbled murrelets and sea otters? Who should be responsible for bringing back the salmon?

For hundreds of years people have used the resources of the coast—its animals, plants, and oil without much thought or understanding of how our needs and behavior affected these resources and the coastal ecosystem. We are now beginning to understand the extent of the damage we have caused. And we are beginning to repair, restore, recover, and protect what is left. These efforts are costly, but more and more money is being spent each year—mostly by taxpayers—to ensure we keep our living planet full of life. The management of the kelp forest and every other part of the coastal ecosystem requires teams of experts. It requires marine mammalogists to watch whales, ornithologists to track murrelets, forestry biologists to assess the health of trees, wildlife managers to follow bear populations, fish biologists to count spawning salmon, and restoration ecologists to replant coastal trees and other vegetation. And it takes a large population of nonexperts—people who want to take care of our coastal resources. People play an important role in the balance of nature, and we share the responsibility of taking care of the Pacific coast and all of our ecosystems. But we must take steps now before the last murrelet disappears in the fog or the last salmon swims out to sea.

When the tide goes out, these students move in to explore the tide pool community. Learning about the Pacific coast ecosystem can be fun, but understanding how to preserve and protect it is hard work that requires everyone's help.

Glossary

adaptation the special features that help organisms survive in a particular environment.

anadromous entering rivers from the ocean to swim upstream. Salmon are an anadromous fish.

biodiversity the variety of plant and animal species in an area.

biological community all of the organisms that live together and interact in a particular environment.

brackish water that is partly salty and partly fresh.

competition demand by two or more organisms or different kinds of organisms for an environmental resource in short supply. In the rocky intertidal community, for example, where suitable living space is limited, there is competition between different species of barnacles for space on the rock.

crepuscular active around dawn and dusk. Marbled murrelets are crepuscular birds that fly to and from their nests and the open ocean in the dim light of dawn and dusk.

ecology the study of the relationships among species and their environment. A person who studies ecology is called an ecologist.

ecosystem the association of living things in a biological community, plus its interactions with the nonliving parts of the environment.

food chain a pathway that describes feeding relationships in which one organism is eaten by another organism that is, in turn, eaten by another.

food web the interaction among more than one food chain.

habitat the place that provides all the living and nonliving things that an organism needs to live and grow.

habitat fragmentation the process by which an organism's habitat is reduced or fragmented. The marbled murrelet's habitat is being fragmented as the forests it nests in are cut down.

holdfast the rootlike structure that anchors many varieties of kelp to the rock on the seafloor.

intertidal zone the area along the coast that is alternately covered and uncovered by high and low tides.

migration the regular, seasonal movement of animals from one place to another.

organism a living thing, such as a plant, animal, or fungus.

photosynthesis the process by which plants and some other organisms that have chlorophyll use sunlight, carbon dioxide, and water to make sugars and other substances.

phytoplankton tiny floating plants. Also known as algae, they create their own energy from the sun and provide food for many other organisms in the food chain.

predator an animal that hunts and kills other animals for food.

primary consumer an animal that eats plants.

producer an organism (generally a plant) that uses energy from the sun to create sugars that animals can use as food.

secondary consumer an animal that feeds on another animal.

stipe the thick stem of a kelp.

subtidal zone the area of the coastal waters that is not exposed by low tides.

Further Exploration

Books and Articles

Carson, Rachel. *The Edge of the Sea*. Boston: Houghton Mifflin, 1998.

Coulombe, Deborah. *The Seaside Naturalist*. New York: Simon & Schuster, 1984.

Kricher, John. *Peterson First Guides: Seashore*. Boston: Houghton-Mifflin, 1992.

McConnaughey, Bayard and Evelyn. *National Audubon Society Nature Guide: Pacific Coast*. New York: Alfred A. Knopf, 1998.

Meinkoth, Norman. *National Aubudon Society Field Guide to North American Seashore Creatures*. New York: Alfred A. Knopf, 1981.

Paine, Stefani. *The World of the Sea Otter*. San Francisco: Sierra Club Books, 1993.

Ricketts, Edward F., and Jack Cavin. *Between Pacific Tides*. Palo Alto, CA: Stanford University Press, 1968.

Steinbeck, John. *Cannery Row*. New York: Penguin, 1993.

Van Dyk, Jere. "Long Journey of the Pacific Salmon," *National Geographic*, July 1990.

Wertheim, Anne. *The Intertidal Wilderness*. San Francisco: Sierra Club Books, 1982.

Wokomir, Richard. "The Fragile Recovery of the California Sea Otter." *National Geographic*, June 1995

Wu, Norbert. *Beneath the Waves: Exploring the Hidden World of the Kelp Forest*. San Francisco: Chronicle Books, 1992.

On the Web

www.epa.gov/owow

www.response.restoration.noaa.gov/kids/kids.html

www.pbs.org/oceanrealm/intheschool/index/html

Organizations

Center for Marine Conservation
1725 DeSales St. NW
Washington, DC 20036
(202) 429-5609
www.cmc-ocean.org

Monterey Bay National Marine Sanctuary
299 Foam St. Suite D
Monterey, CA 93940
(408) 647-4201
http://bonita.mbnms.nos.noaa.gov

Oregon Parks and Recreation Department
South Coast
10965 Cape Arago Hwy.
Coos Bay, OR 97420
(800) 551-6949
www.prd.state.or.us/home/html

Prairie Creek Redwoods State Park
Orick, Ca 95555
(707) 464-6101
www.nps.gov.redw/

Index

Page numbers for illustrations are in **boldface**.